ROCK GUITAR CLASSICS

Play Along with 8 Great-Sounding Tracks

T0041114

BOOK & PLAY-ALONG CD

WITH **TNT** TONE 'N' TEMPO CHANGER

About the TNT Changer

Use the TNT software to change keys, loop playback, and mute tracks for play-along. For complete instructions, see the **TnT ReadMe.pdf** file on your enhanced CD.

Windows users: insert the CD into your computer, double-click on My Computer, right-click on your CD drive icon, and select Explore to locate the file.

Mac users: insert the CD into your computer and double-click on the CD icon on your desktop to locate the file.

Produced by
Alfred Music Publishing Co., Inc.
P.O. Box 10003
Van Nuys, CA 91410-0003
alfred.com

Printed in USA.

ISBN-10: 0-7390-8270-1 (Book & CD)
ISBN-13: 978-0-7390-8270-6 (Book & CD)

Cover photo: © Rolf Adlercreutz

 Alfred Cares. Contents printed on 100% recycled paper.

Contents

ANOTHER BRICK IN THE WALL (PART 2)

Words and Music by
ROGER WATERS

*2nd time sung by children's chorus 8va.
**Elec. Gtrs. 1 & 2 tacet 1st two measures, 2nd time.

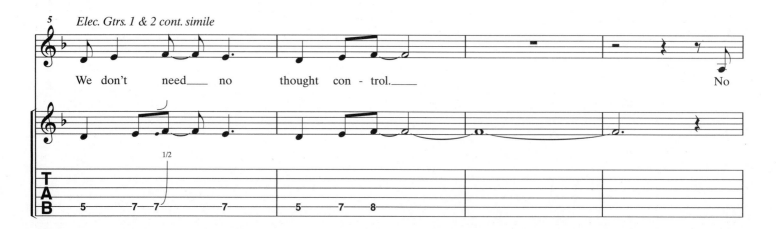

Another Brick in the Wall (Part 2) - 6 - 1

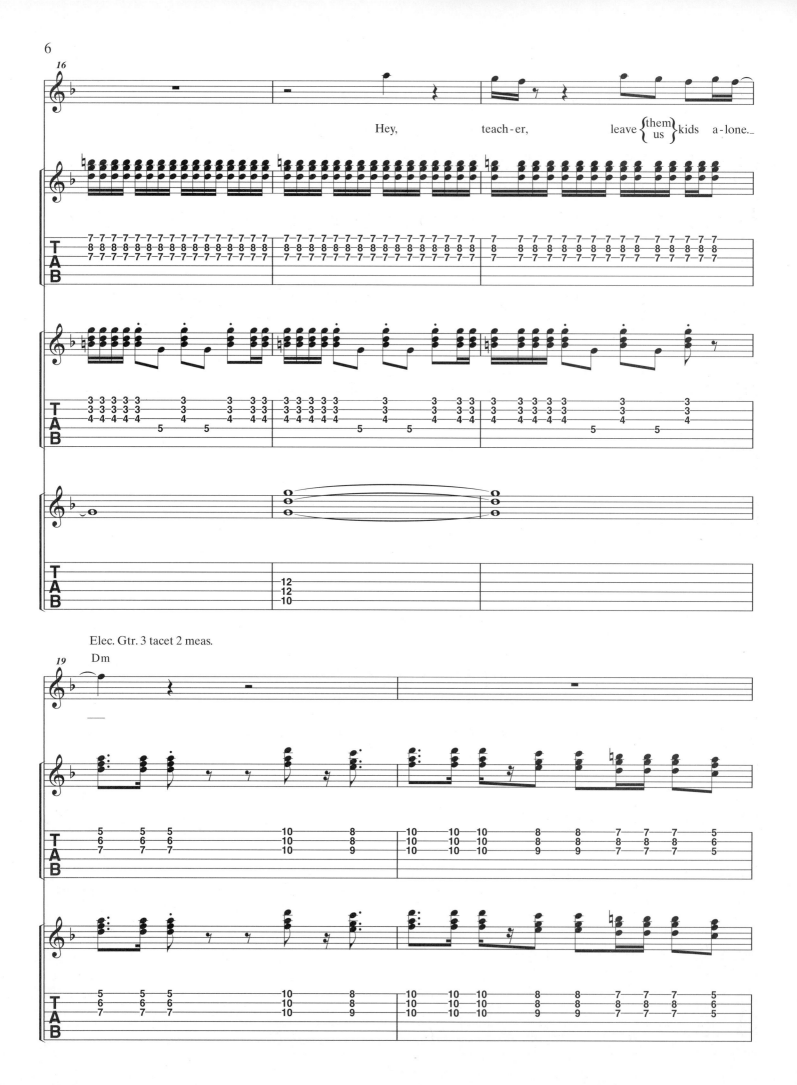

Hey,   teach - er,   leave {them us} kids   a - lone._

Elec. Gtr. 3 tacet 2 meas.

Dm

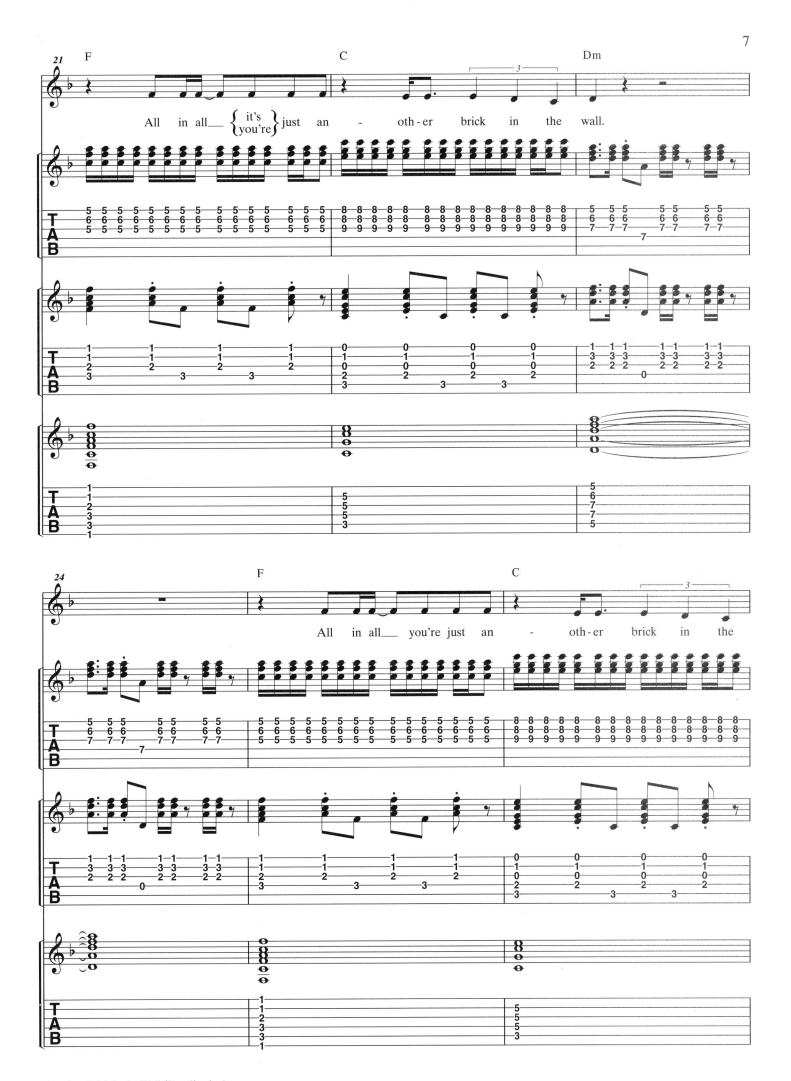

8

Outro: Repeat ad lib. and fade
Band tacet, drums only.
N.C.

DON'T STOP BELIEVIN'

Words and Music by
JONATHAN CAIN, NEAL SCHON
and STEVE PERRY

12

Verse 3:

Elec. Gtrs. 1 & 2 tacet

A sing-er in a smok-y room.___ The smell of wine and cheap per - fume._____

For a smile_ they can share the night;_ it goes on and on___ and on___ and on.___

% *Bridge:*

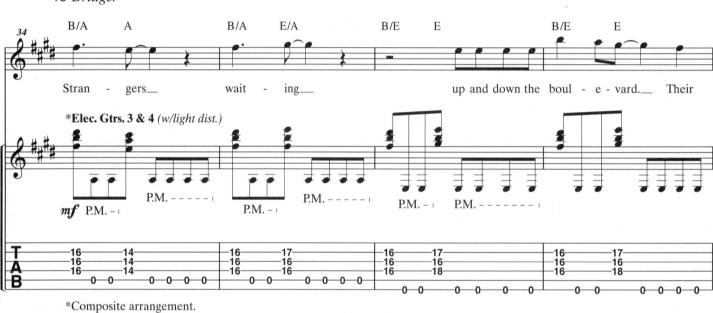

Stran - gers___ wait - ing___ up and down the boul - e - vard.___ Their

*Composite arrangement.

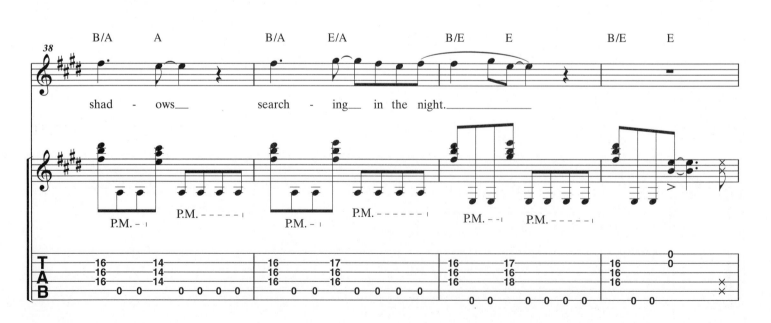

shad - ows___ search - ing_ in the night._____

Verse 4:

Verse 5:

⊕ Coda

Guitar Solo:

w/Rhy. Figs. 1 *(Elec. Gtr. 3)* **& 1A** *(Elec. Gtr. 4)*

HONKY TONK WOMEN

Elec. Gtrs. 1 & 2 in Open G tuning:
⑥ = D ③ = G
⑤ = G ② = B
④ = D ① = D

Words and Music by
MICK JAGGER and KEITH RICHARDS

Moderately ♩ = 117

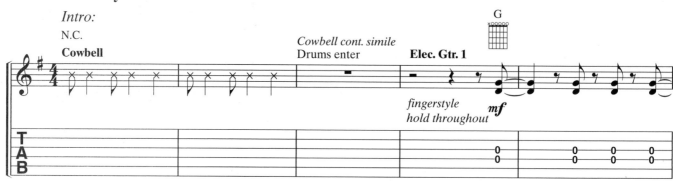

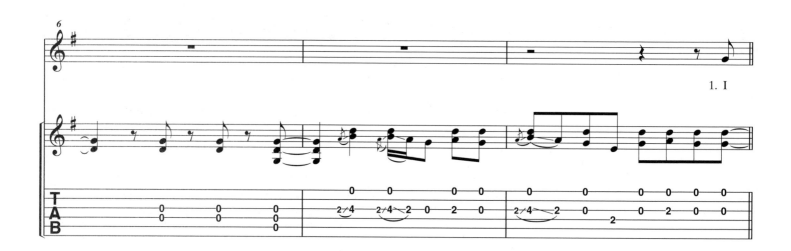

met a gin-soaked bar-room queen in Mem - phis. She
(2.) laid a di-vor-cée in New York Cit - y. I

Honky Tonk Women - 6 - 1

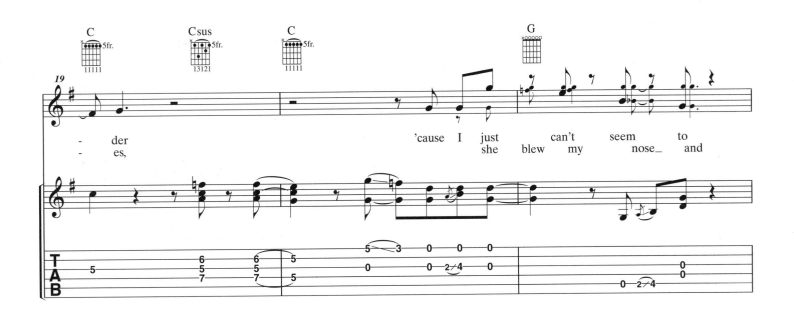

Chorus:

22

EUROPA
(Earth's Cry Heaven's Smile)

Words and Music by
CARLOS SANTANA and TOM COSTER

Europa (Earth's Cry Heaven's Smile) - 7 - 3

28

Europa (Earth's Cry Heaven's Smile) - 7 - 6

LOSING MY RELIGION

Words and Music by
WILLIAM BERRY, PETER BUCK,
MICHAEL MILLS and MICHAEL STIPE

Verse:

34

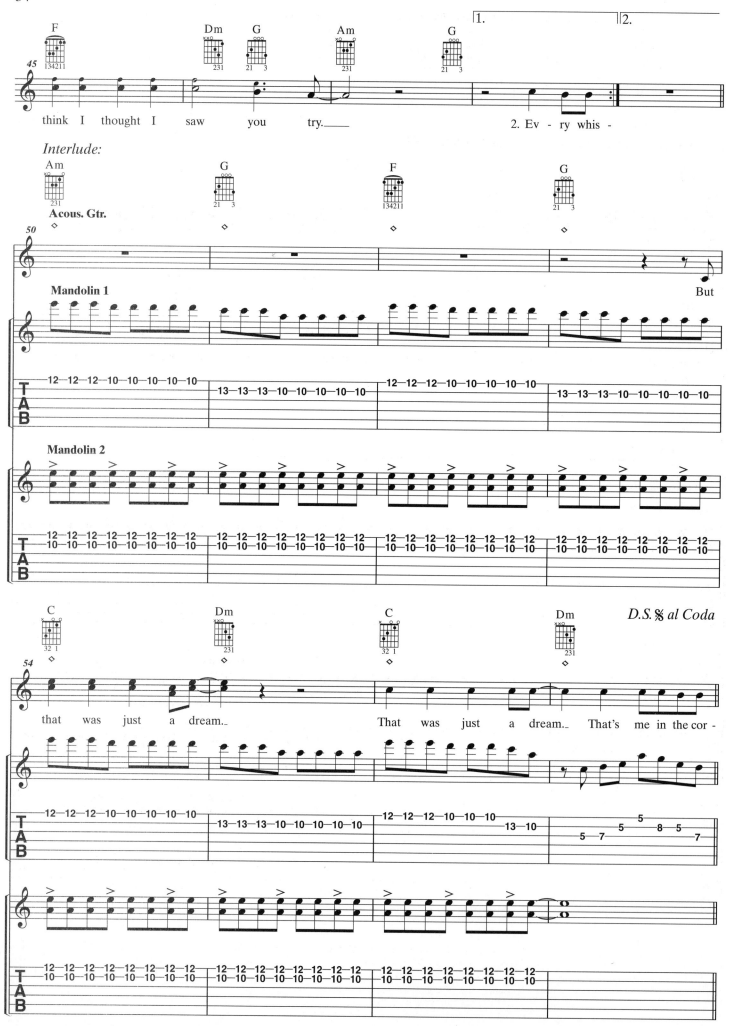

Verse 2:
Every whisper of every hour
I'm choosing my confession, trying to keep an eye on you,
Like a hurt lost and blinded fool, fool.
Oh no, I've said too much, I set it up.
Consider this; consider this, the hint of the century; consider this.
The slip that brought me to my knees failed.
What if all these fantasies come flailing around?
Now I've said too much.
(To Chorus:)

ROCK AND ROLL ALL NITE

Words and Music by
PAUL STANLEY and GENE SIMMONS

*All gtrs. tuned down 1/2 step:
⑥ = E♭ ③ = G♭
⑤ = A♭ ② = B♭
④ = D♭ ① = E♭

Moderately ♩ = 142

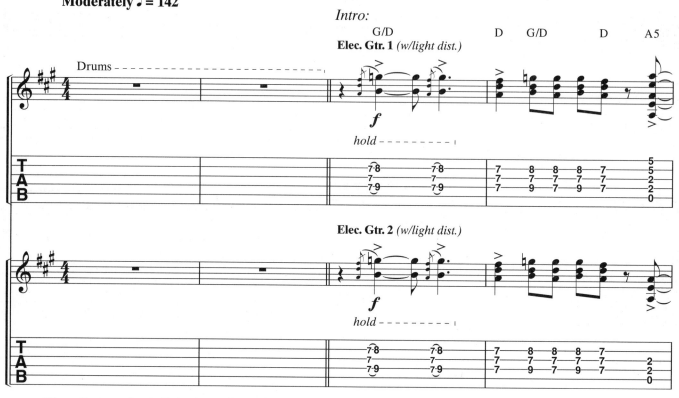

*Recording sounds a half step lower than written.

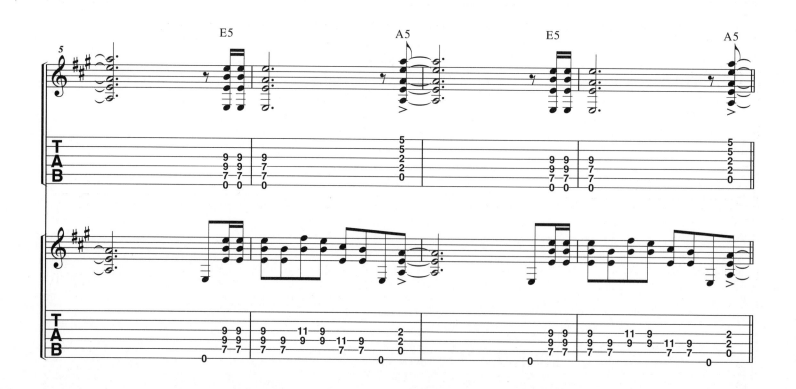

Rock and Roll All Nite - 8 - 1

Verse:

1. You show us ev - 'ry - thing you've got,____
2. You keep on say - ing you'll be mine for a while,____

you keep on danc - ing and the room gets hot.
you're look - ing fan - cy and I like your style.

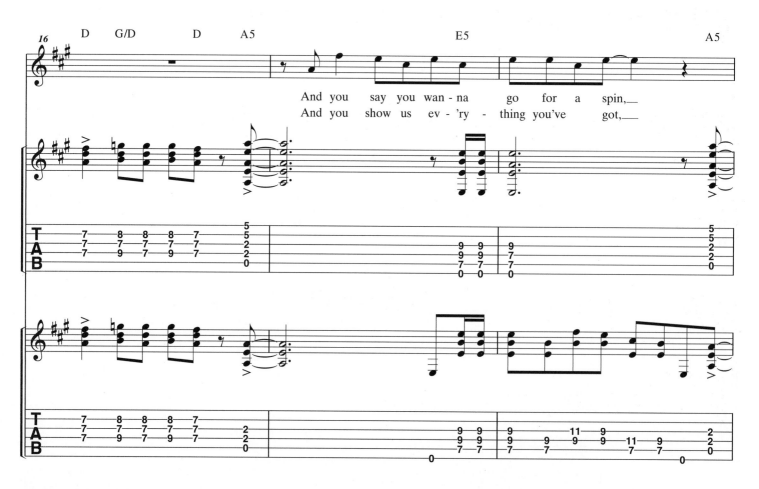

Rock and Roll All Night - 8 - 4

Guitar Solo:

ROCK AND ROLL

Words and Music by
JIMMY PAGE, ROBERT PLANT,
JOHN PAUL JONES and JOHN BONHAM

Briskly ♩ = 165

A *Intro:*
A7
Elec. Gtrs. 1 & 2 *(w/dist.)*
Rhy. Fig. 1

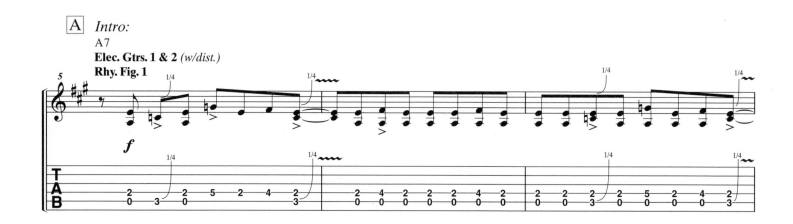

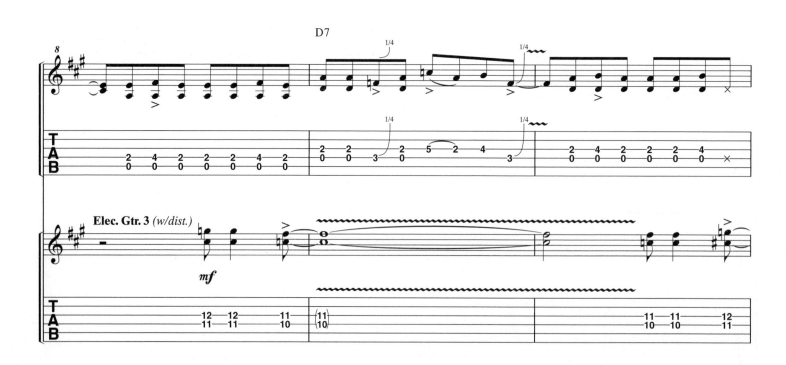

Rock and Roll - 11 - 1

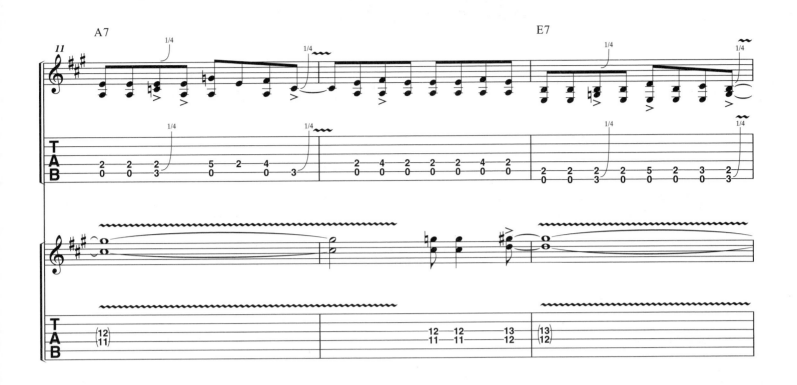

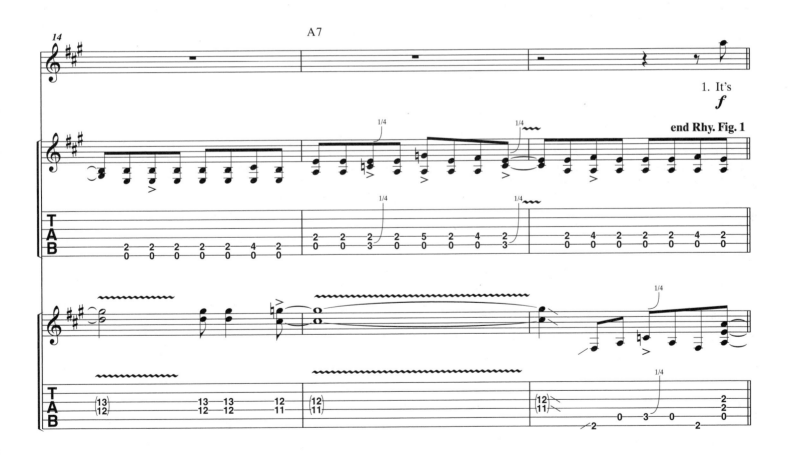

1. It's

f

end Rhy. Fig. 1

B Verses 1 & 2:

been a long time since I rock and rolled._____ It's
been a long time since the book of love._____ I

Elec. Gtrs. 1 & 2

been a long time since I did the stroll._____
can't count the tears of a life with no love._____

Ooh, let me get it back, let me get it back, let me get it
Ah, car - ry me back, car - ry me back, car - ry me back,

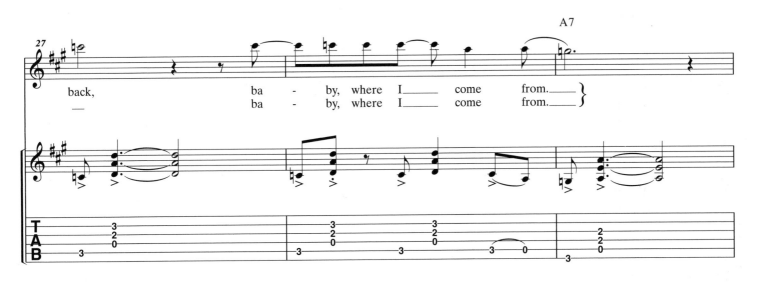

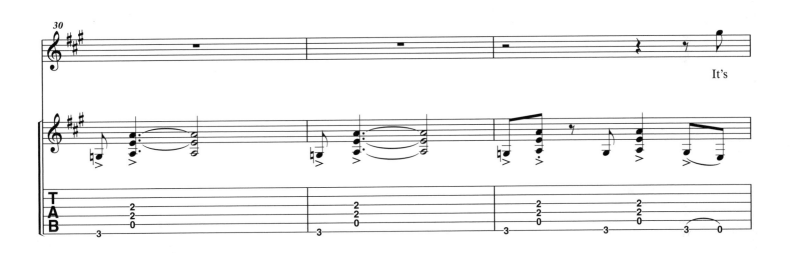

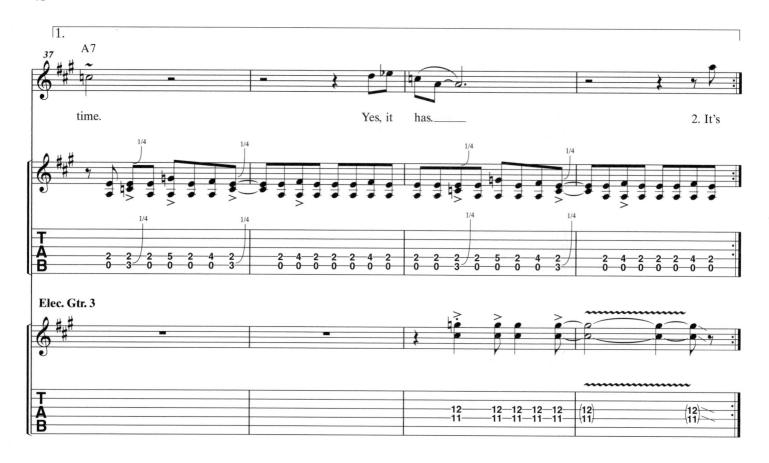

1.

time.   Yes, it has._____   2. It's

Elec. Gtr. 3

2.

time.

Aww._____

Elec. Gtr. 3

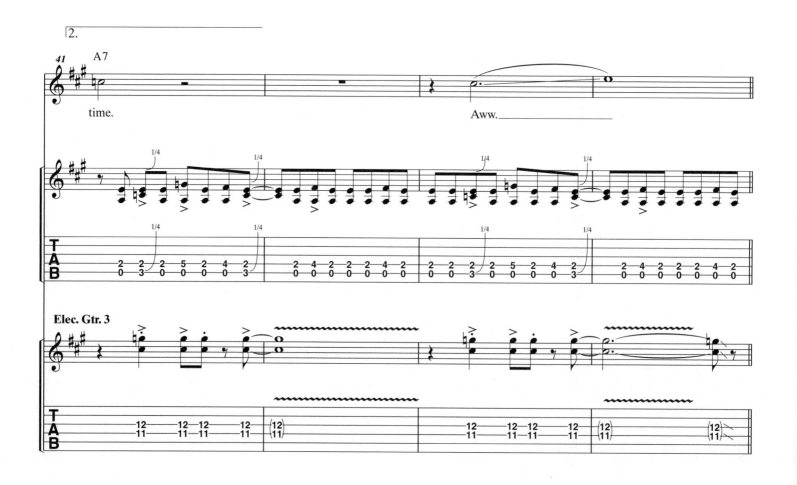

D *Interlude:*
w/Rhy. Fig. 1 *(Elec. Gtrs. 1 & 2)*

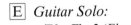

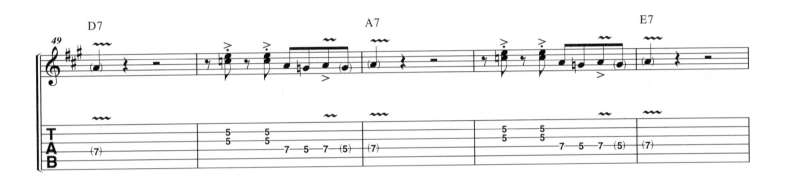

*Notes in parens generated by tape echo.

E *Guitar Solo:*
w/Rhy. Fig. 2 *(Elec. Gtrs. 1 & 2)*

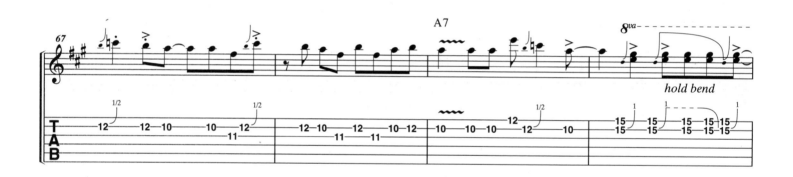

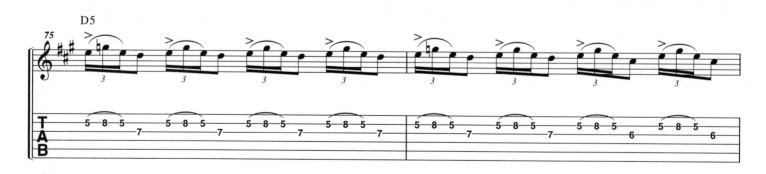

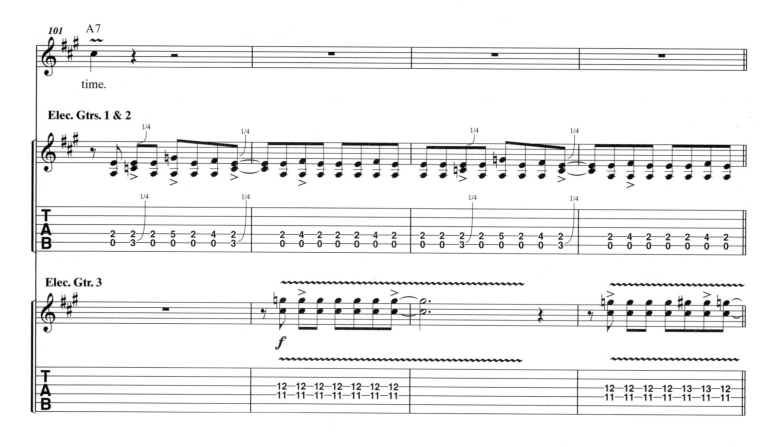

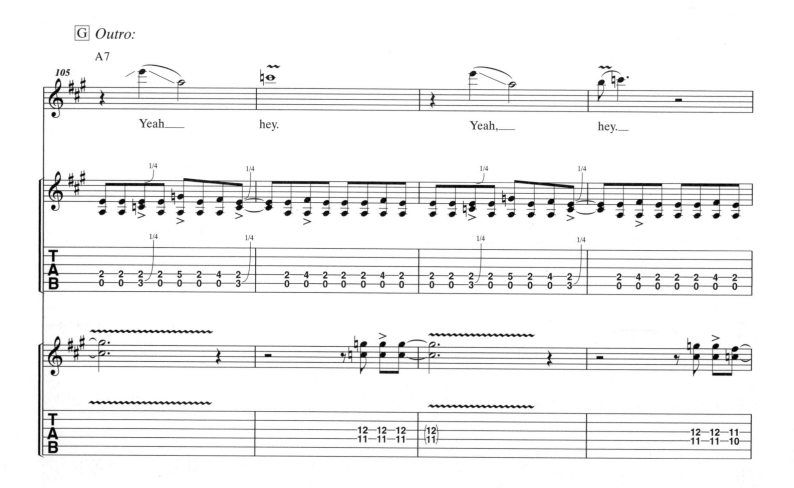

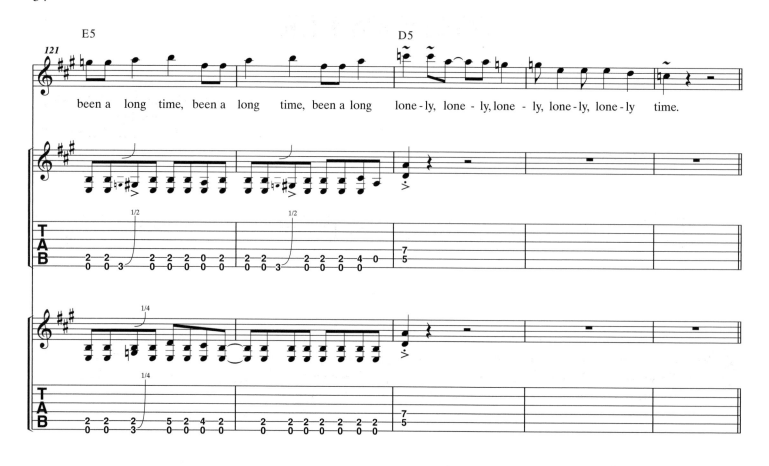

been a long time, been a long time, been a long lone-ly, lone-ly, lone-ly, lone-ly, lone-ly time.

(free tempo)
Drums
On cue

TOM SAWYER

Words by
PYE DUBOIS and NEIL PEART
Music by
GEDDY LEE and ALEX LIFESON

Moderately ♩ = 87.5

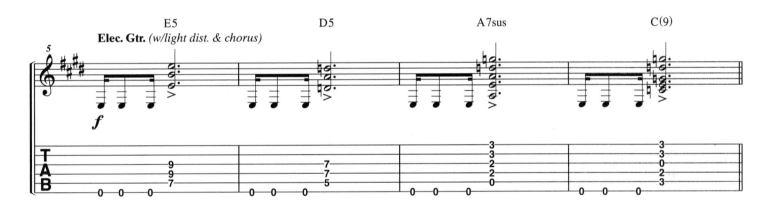

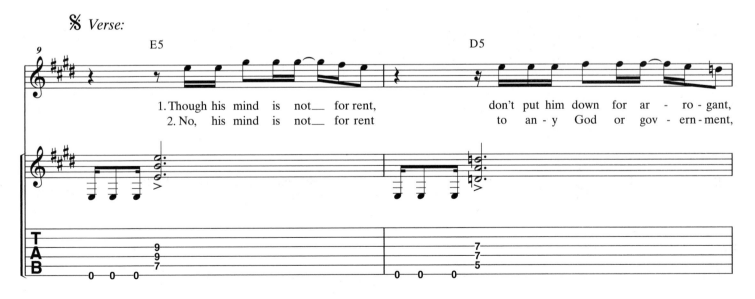

Tom Sawyer - 7 - 1

58

Tom Sawyer - 7 - 5

TABLATURE EXPLANATION
TAB illustrates the six strings of the guitar.
Notes and chords are indicated by the placement of fret numbers on each string.

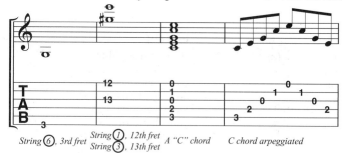

String ⑥, 3rd fret   String ①, 12th fret   A "C" chord   C chord arpeggiated
              String ③, 13th fret

BENDING NOTES

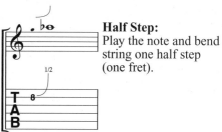

Half Step:
Play the note and bend string one half step (one fret).

Whole Step:
Play the note and bend string one whole step (two frets).

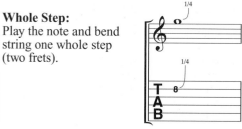

Slight Bend/ Quarter-Tone Bend:
Play the note and bend string sharp.

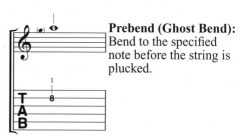

Prebend (Ghost Bend):
Bend to the specified note before the string is plucked.

Prebend and Release:
Play the already-bent string, then immediately drop it down to the fretted note.

Unison Bend:
Play both notes and immediately bend the lower note to the same pitch as the higher note.

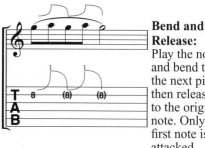

Bend and Release:
Play the note and bend to the next pitch, then release to the original note. Only the first note is attacked.

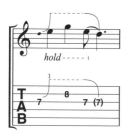

Bends Involving More Than One String:
Play the note and bend the string while playing an additional note on another string. Upon release, relieve the pressure from the additional note allowing the original note to sound alone.

Bends Involving Stationary Notes:
Play both notes and immediately bend the lower note up to pitch. Release bend as indicated.

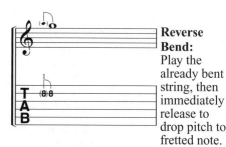

Reverse Bend:
Play the already bent string, then immediately release to drop pitch to fretted note.

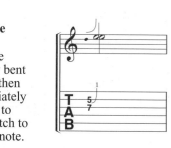

Unison Bend:
Play both notes and immediately bend the lower note to the same pitch as the higher note.

Double Note Bend:
Play both notes and immediately bend both strings simultaneously up the indicated intervals.

ARTICULATIONS

Hammer On (Ascending Slur): Play the lower note, then "hammer" your finger to the higher note. Only the first note is plucked.

Pull Off (Descending Slur): Play the higher note with your first finger already in position on the lower note. Pull your finger off the first note with a strong downward motion that plucks the string—sounding the lower note.

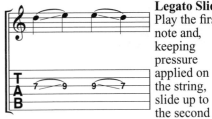

Legato Slide: Play the first note and, keeping pressure applied on the string, slide up to the second note. The diagonal line shows that it is a slide and not a hammer-on or a pull-off.

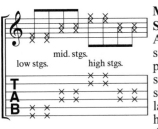

Muted Strings: A percussive sound is produced by striking the strings while laying the fret hand across them.

Palm Mute: The notes are muted (muffled) by placing the palm of the pick hand lightly on the strings, just in front of the bridge.

Left Hand Hammer: Using only the left hand, hammer on the first note played on each string.

Glissando: Play note and slide in specified direction.

Bend and Tap Technique: Play note and bend to specified interval. While holding bend, tap onto fret indicated with a "t."

Fretboard Tapping: Tap onto the note indicated by the "t" with a finger of the pick hand, then pull off to the following note held by the fret hand.

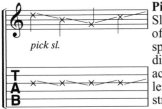

Pick Slide: Slide the edge of the pick in specified direction across the length of the strings.

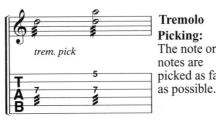

Tremolo Picking: The note or notes are picked as fast as possible.

Trill: Hammer on and pull off consecutively and as fast as possible between the original note and the grace note.

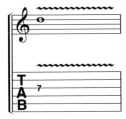

Vibrato: The pitch of a note is varied by a rapid shaking of the fret-hand finger, wrist, and forearm.

Accent: Notes or chords are to be played with added emphasis.

Staccato (Detached Notes): Notes or chords are to be played about half their noted value and with separation.

HARMONICS

  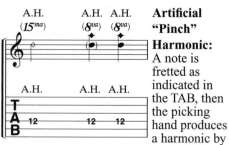

Natural Harmonic:
A finger of the fret hand lightly touches the string at the note indicated in the TAB and is plucked by the pick producing a bell-like sound called a harmonic.

Artificial Harmonic:
Fret the note at the first TAB number, lightly touch the string at the fret indicated in parens (usually 12 frets higher than the fretted note), then pluck the string with an available finger or your pick.

Artificial "Pinch" Harmonic:
A note is fretted as indicated in the TAB, then the picking hand produces a harmonic by squeezing the pick firmly while using the tip of the index finger in the pick attack. If parenthesis are found around the fretted note, it does not sound. No parenthesis means both the fretted note and the A.H. are heard simultaneously.

RHYTHM SLASHES

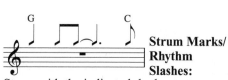 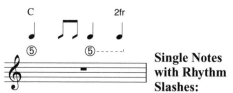

Strum Marks/ Rhythm Slashes:
Strum with the indicated rhythm pattern. Strum marks can be located above the staff or within the staff.

Single Notes with Rhythm Slashes:
Sometimes single notes are incorporated into a strum pattern. The circled number below is the string and the fret number is above.

TREMOLO BAR

 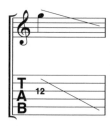

Specified Interval:
The pitch of a note or chord is lowered to the specified interval and then return as indicated. The action of the tremolo bar is graphically represented by the peaks and valleys of the diagram.

Unspecified Interval:
The pitch of a note or chord is lowered, usually very dramatically, until the pitch of the string becomes indeterminate.

PICK DIRECTION

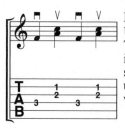

Downstrokes and Upstrokes:
The downstroke is indicated with this symbol (∏) and the upstroke is indicated with this (V).